Original title:
Silent Snow

Copyright © 2024 Swan Charm
All rights reserved.

Author: Liisi Lendorav
ISBN HARDBACK: 978-9916-79-777-8
ISBN PAPERBACK: 978-9916-79-778-5
ISBN EBOOK: 978-9916-79-779-2

Evaporating Footprints on White

A silent trail on snowy plains,
Each step a tale, soon lost in rains.
Whispers of journeys left behind,
Fading softly, gentle, kind.

They vanish quick, like morning dew,
Turning to mist as dreams pursue.
Ghosts of laughter fading fast,
In winter's grip, we breathe the past.

Ghostly Patterns in the Air

Ethereal shapes in twilight's breath,
Dance through shadows, whispering death.
Winds of stories drift and weave,
Tracing secrets, we believe.

On a canvas of fading night,
Specters swirl, a haunting flight.
Silhouettes of things once known,
In silence bound, yet not alone.

The Embrace of a Winter's Whisper

Softly falls the silver snow,
Blanketing earth in a gentle glow.
Winter's breath, a tender call,
Wrapping all in a silent thrall.

Whispers weave through branches bare,
Murmurs float on frigid air.
In this stillness, hearts ignite,
Finding warmth in coldest night.

Shimmering Dust on Sleeping Grounds

A glimmer rests where shadows lie,
Underneath the starlit sky.
Scattered dreams, like sparkles lost,
Caught in slumber, free of cost.

Each twinkle tells a story deep,
Of hopes we guard, of love we keep.
On sleeping grounds, the silence hums,
While in the dark, the laughter comes.

Whirls of Snowshine Float By

Whirls of snowshine in the night,
Twinkling softly, pure and bright.
Gentle breezes softly play,
As the world drifts far away.

Silence wraps the earth in peace,
Sparkling flakes, a sweet release.
Underneath the moon's soft glow,
Magic dances in the snow.

Each flake a story, unique,
In the stillness, softly speak.
Nature's wonder, here we find,
Whirls of snowflakes, intertwined.

Frost-kissed branches, night's embrace,
Time stands still in this sweet space.
Footprints vanish in the white,
Lost in dreams of endless night.

The Elegance of a Winter's Hush

In the elegance of winter's hush,
Snowflakes fall in softest brush.
Every twig and leaf adorned,
By nature's grace, silently formed.

Whispers linger in the air,
Frozen moments, rich and rare.
A quiet beauty reigns this night,
As shadows blend with soft twilight.

All around, the world feels new,
Wrapped in diamonds, sparkling dew.
Crisp and clear, the stars ignite,
Guiding dreams through the night.

Stillness deepens, hearts awake,
In this wonder, none forsake.
Moments cherished, shared with care,
The elegance in winter's air.

A Thousand Whispers in the Air

A thousand whispers in the air,
As winter weaves without a care.
Rustling leaves and distant calls,
Nature's symphony that enthralls.

Each breath carries tales untold,
Of frosty nights and joys of old.
Embers glow in twilight gray,
Memories linger, never sway.

Seasons shift, yet still remain,
Every heartbeat, every strain.
Through the chill, warm spirits rise,
Underneath the starlit skies.

In this wonder, hearts unite,
As shadows blend with soft moonlight.
A thousand whispers softly play,
Carrying dreams along the way.

The Stillness That Follows

The stillness that follows the storm,
Leaves the world in perfect form.
Crystals linger on the ground,
Nature's peace in silence found.

Softly now, the daylight breaks,
Painting hues, the morning wakes.
Every corner, bright and clear,
As the warmth of day draws near.

Footprints echo in the snow,
Memories held, as breezes blow.
In the calm, new hopes arise,
Underneath the vast, blue skies.

Time moves on, yet still we cling,
To the gifts that winter brings.
The stillness that follows, we crave,
In its quiet, we are saved.

A Shroud of Gentle Peace

Amidst the whispering trees,
A gentle breeze unfolds,
Carrying dreams with ease,
In her arms, the world holds.

Silence drapes the ground,
A soft quilt of white snow,
Nature's grace profound,
In her calm, we all grow.

Stars twinkle in the night,
A blanket of twinkling lights,
Guiding hearts toward right,
In the stillness, ignites.

Each breath a quiet prayer,
Easing burdens we bear,
In every soft, sweet layer,
Moments tender and rare.

Peace wraps around like night,
Cradling our weary souls,
In her soothing light,
Harmony gently rolls.

Frostflakes Danced in Quiet

Through the window, they glide,
Frostflakes twirl with grace,
In the stillness, they bide,
Whispers in a soft space.

Each flake a fleeting dream,
Delicate as the night,
In silver, they softly gleam,
A ballet of pure light.

Falling in perfect time,
Music of the cold air,
Nature's gentle rhyme,
Dancing without a care.

Wrapped in a winter hug,
Time seems to stand still,
Life, a tender tug,
Nature's magic to fulfill.

As shadows start to play,
Frostflakes kiss the ground,
In their soft ballet,
Joy in silence is found.

The Lullaby of Falling Flakes

As day melts into night,
The sky dons a white veil,
Each flake a soft delight,
A calming winter tale.

They swirl in whispered dreams,
A hush across the land,
Filling hearts with moonbeams,
As peace takes gentle hand.

Lullabies of the cold,
Wrapped in a frosty breath,
Stories soft and bold,
In the cradle of death.

Gentle breezes arise,
Holding each flake so dear,
Under vast, starry skies,
Winter's magic draws near.

Each flake a whispered song,
Carried by the night air,
In their dance, we belong,
Finding warmth everywhere.

Muffled Footsteps on Pure Ground

Through the white, we wander,
Each step a muted sound,
Lost in thoughts, we ponder,
On this soft, sacred ground.

Footprints in silence trace,
Stories told without words,
A peaceful, timeless space,
Where our spirit reverts.

The forest stands so still,
Wrapped in a frosty shroud,
A canvas of pure will,
Nature's beauty, proud.

Muffled laughter and cheer,
Cries of joy gently fade,
In the crisp air, we're here,
Memories softly made.

As we tread on this snow,
Hearts full of warmth and love,
In this tranquil glow,
Guided from above.

Shadows Beneath the Snow

Pale whispers weave through trees,
Shadows shift beneath the frost.
Silhouettes of what once stood,
Nature holds its breath, embossed.

Snowflakes dance on winter's breath,
Each a tale of silent nights.
Beneath the weight of purest white,
Life awaits the spring's first sights.

Footprints mark the quiet ground,
Where the hidden creatures tread.
Softly gathered all around,
Silent dreams in pillow bed.

Branches bow with silver tears,
Hushed beneath their frozen crowns.
Echoes of forgotten years,
Whimper through the winter towns.

In the stillness of the cold,
Time forgets its hurried pace.
Stories whispered, untold gold,
Waiting for the sun to chase.

The Invisible Chorus of Winter

Brittle notes in frigid air,
Nature croons with icy grace.
Every flake a soft refrain,
Filling each forgotten space.

Wind caresses all it sees,
Singing through the barren trees.
Frosted breath, a muted song,
Carried where the shadows flee.

Underneath the silver skies,
Harmonies of hush abide.
Winter's magic, unseen ties,
Binding worlds, in silence, wide.

Moonlight glimmers on the snow,
Softly lighting every curve.
A lullaby, serene and slow,
In the night, our hearts preserve.

Though the world appears so still,
Life's crescendo waits within.
Echoes of a springtime thrill,
Whispered hopes, where dreams begin.

A Quiet Thaw Approaches

Beneath the snow, soft stirrings lie,
Tender shoots, the earth's first sigh.
Melting whispers bring the thaw,
Each droplet bears the sun's sweet law.

Glistening on the branches bare,
Icicles drape without a care.
Daylight warms the frozen ground,
Promises of life abound.

Gentle breezes start to play,
Shaking off the winter's gray.
Underneath the blanket cold,
Nature wakes to tales retold.

With every drop, the heartbeat stirs,
Life returns as spring prefers.
Colors bloom from beneath the white,
Bursting forth in pure delight.

Soon the world will wear a dress,
Adorned in blooms, a sweet excess.
Hearts will dance, and laughter flow,
In the moments where thaw starts to show.

Blanketed in Soft Light

Morning breaks with tender rays,
Cascading through the wintry haze.
Snowflakes shimmer, crystal bright,
A world reborn in soft light.

Silence drapes the sleepy ground,
Nature's peace in whispers found.
Every corner, dressed in white,
Captures moments, pure delight.

Trees stand tall in shimmering coats,
Guardians of the dreams they wrote.
Underneath their frosted crowns,
Lies a quiet, sacred ground.

A canvas wide, the artist's hand,
Crafting scenes both grand and bland.
Softly painted, all in sight,
Life awakens, blanketed light.

With each breath, the winter sighs,
In the glow of morning skies.
Hope ignites in every flake,
As the day begins to wake.

Snowflakes' Soft Secrets

Glistening whispers in the air,
They dance like dreams, so light and rare.
Each flake a story, fresh and new,
In winter's breath, they twirl and skew.

Silent secrets they softly spill,
Falling gently, a magic thrill.
Nature's quilt unfolds with grace,
A crystal world, a pure embrace.

Under moonlight, their shimmer bright,
Transforming shadows into light.
Each drift and swirl, a fleeting sigh,
In frozen realms where time slips by.

Stillness Beneath the Frozen Sky

The world freezes, in muted hues,
Wrapped in blankets of frosted blues.
Tall trees wear crowns of glistening white,
While stars twinkle in the velvet night.

Silence reigns, a tranquil song,
The evening air feels calm and strong.
Breath of winter, crisp and clear,
Whispers echo, drawing near.

Footsteps crunch on snow-laden ground,
In this stillness, peace is found.
With every flake, nature's delight,
A quiet world, serene and bright.

Dusk Falls on a Snowy Canvas

The sun dips low, a fiery glow,
Painting shadows in the snow.
Pastel skies, a soft descent,
A masterpiece in twilight spent.

Hues of pink and shades of gold,
As winter tales begin to unfold.
The chill embraces, a gentle call,
While day gives way to night's soft fall.

Snowflakes shimmer in fading light,
Transforming darkness into bright.
Each moment brief, yet pure and true,
A canvas brushed with evening's hue.

A Symphony of Winter's Quiet

In this hush, the world holds its breath,
As winter lays all life to rest.
Softly drifts of white cascade,
An orchestra where silence played.

Branches bow with a crystal crown,
Nature's beauty, gently wound.
The air is crisp, the night serene,
In this stillness, peace is seen.

Moonlight casts a gentle glow,
Upon the earth, a silver show.
Harmony sings with every flake,
A soothing balm, as stillness wakes.

A Caress from Above

Softly the sunlight breaks,
Like a whisper of sweet grace.
Kissing the earth with warmth,
As shadows begin to chase.

Gentle breezes dance and twirl,
Through fields of golden wheat.
Nature's breath begins to stir,
In a rhythm, pure and sweet.

Clouds drift by, a cotton quilt,
Adorning the sky's vast dome.
Every flutter, every lilt,
Feels like a lover's home.

Mountains loom, majestic, bold,
Guardians of this sacred land.
In their presence, tales unfold,
Of the beauty they withstand.

In every morn, a promise bright,
Of hope and love that never fail.
A caress from the day's soft light,
In whispered breaths, the heart exhales.

Twilight's Whispering White

In twilight's gentle embrace,
The world cloaked in silver light.
Shadows stretch and softly trace,
As day surrenders to the night.

Whispers float on twilight air,
Like secrets shared between two.
Stars blink softly, unaware,
Of the dreams that soon ensue.

The moon, a guardian bright,
Bathes the earth in its glow.
Casting shadows, soft and light,
Where hidden wonders start to show.

Branches sway in a soft tune,
As night creatures start to play.
The silver beams of a bright moon,
Guide the lost along their way.

In twilight's dance, peace prevails,
Wrapped in dreams of whispered flight.
A world where love never fails,
In twilight's whispering white.

Still Waters of Frost's Grace

On still waters, silent gleam,
Frost paints delicate white lace.
Nature stirs, a frozen dream,
Captured in this calm embrace.

Trees wear coats of crystal bright,
Reflecting dusk's soft sigh.
In this world of silent night,
The stars gaze down from high.

A gentle hush blankets the air,
As time slows in its grace.
Each moment, a treasure rare,
In nature's peaceful space.

Ripples break the quiet calm,
Drawing goosebumps on the skin
Cool whispers hold a healing balm,
As night begins to spin.

Still waters cradle frozen dreams,
In their tranquil, icy hold.
A scene crafted from whispered themes,
Revealed in silver and gold.

Echoes in a Blanket of Ice

In the hush of winter's breath,
Echoes bounce from tree to tree.
Nature speaks in frozen depth,
Where silence holds its jubilee.

Footsteps crunch on powdered snow,
A melody of crisp delight.
As shadows dance, they come and go,
In the embrace of gentle night.

Each flake, a tale of its own,
Falling softly from above.
Wrapped in frost, the world has grown,
In splendor wrapped in silent love.

Branches arch, adorned with grace,
A crystal chorus fills the sky.
Nature sings in this still space,
A winter's hymn, a soft goodbye.

In a blanket of ice, dreams rest,
Whispers echo through the trees.
A tranquil heart feels truly blessed,
In the stillness, found in ease.

Serenity's Frozen Touch

In the silence of the night,
Snowflakes dance and swirl so light.
They blanket dreams with gentle grace,
Whispering secrets of this place.

Moonlight drapes the world in white,
Stars above, a twinkling sight.
Each breath carries a chill so sweet,
Nature's hush beneath our feet.

Frozen streams glisten like glass,
Time slows down, as moments pass.
In this realm where peace resides,
Serenity's beauty gently guides.

Amidst the stillness, hearts align,
In every crystal, stories shine.
We find a refuge in the calm,
Wrapped in winter's soothing balm.

Embrace the quiet, let it flow,
In each flake, a tranquil glow.
With every heartbeat, cherish much,
The quiet magic of its touch.

Veils of Tranquility

Mist rolls in, soft and light,
Hiding the dawn, a gentle sight.
Nature's breath, a whisper low,
Through the trees, the secrets flow.

Lakes reflect the waking skies,
Where silence holds the softest sighs.
Every ripple, a fleeting chance,
To lose ourselves in nature's dance.

Petals fall with graceful ease,
Rustling softly in the breeze.
Colors blend in sweet embrace,
Crafting calm in every space.

In this haze, we find our muse,
Wrapped in stillness, we refuse
The rush of life, the loud refrain,
Here in veils where peace will reign.

Let the hours drift like clouds,
In tranquil layers, silent shrouds.
We wander through this softened land,
Holding serenity in our hand.

Gentle Murmurs in the Air

Whispers rise with morning light,
Birdsong fills the day with delight.
Breezes carry tales anew,
Nature's voice, soft and true.

Leaves flutter in a gentle sway,
As shadows dance throughout the day.
Every moment lingers near,
In the symphony we hear.

Clouds drift by, serene and slow,
Casting dreams where we can go.
In the hush, our minds unwind,
Lost in thoughts, so intertwined.

Each soft sound, a soothing balm,
Calming heartbeats, bringing calm.
In the air, we find our peace,
In every whisper, sweet release.

Join the murmurs, feel their grace,
In this wonder, find your place.
Let the echoes guide your way,
Through the gentle light of day.

Soft Footfalls on Gleaming Ground

Footfalls tread on dewy grass,
Where the moments gently pass.
Each step carries tales untold,
In this hush, we dare be bold.

Paths awaken with every stride,
Nature's beauty as our guide.
Beneath the arch of oaks so grand,
We weave our dreams across the land.

The morning sun begins to rise,
Painting gold across the skies.
With every step, our spirits soar,
Amongst the whispers of folklore.

Echoes linger, soft and bright,
As shadows dance with pure delight.
Through the trees, we wander free,
In this realm of reverie.

In every soft and gleaming tread,
We find the path that dreams have led.
Let every moment, pure and sound,
Be cherished here on gleaming ground.

The Naive Notes of Winter's Choir

In frosted air, a silence sings,
The world wrapped tight in white embrace.
Soft whispers dance on icy wings,
As winter paints with gentle grace.

Notes of joy on snowflakes fall,
While branches bow with silver dreams.
Nature's breath, a soft enthrall,
In every glint, a magic gleams.

The trees stand tall, adorned in frost,
Each crystal shard, a story new.
A fleeting warmth, we count the cost,
Of days gone by, so fresh and true.

With every gust, a tale unfolds,
Of laughter lost in winter's chill.
The sunlight's touch, a glow that molds,
The heart to hope, the spirit's thrill.

In snow-kissed nights, the stars align,
They shimmer softly, pure and bright.
In the choir's song, we find the sign,
That spring will come, it holds us tight.

Where Cold Meets a Whispered Dream

In the hush of night, the world breathes slow,
A blanket soft, the earth it slows.
The moonlight weaves a silver glow,
Where icy rivers gently flow.

The winds carry secrets through the trees,
Each branch a guardian, old and wise.
With soft caresses, the night agrees,
To cradle dreams beneath the skies.

Frost-kissed fields, a silent dance,
Where shadows play in shades of blue.
In every glance, a fleeting chance,
To hold the warmth, to feel what's true.

As whispers flutter, dreams take flight,
In the cold air, they glide and roam.
A landscape pure, a dreamer's sight,
In winter's heart, we find our home.

Where cold meets warmth, we hum our tune,
In harmony, the stars align.
Underneath the watchful moon,
We find our peace, we intertwine.

Muted Steps Through Winter's Breath

Softly tread on snowy ground,
Whispers echo all around.
Frosty air, a crisp delight,
As day surrenders to the night.

Barren trees in silence stand,
Blanketed by white so grand.
Footprints fade, a fleeting trace,
While winter holds its cold embrace.

The moonlight dances on the snow,
Casting shadows, soft and slow.
A world transformed, so pure, serene,
In muted tones, a tranquil scene.

Breath of winter, hushed and deep,
Secrets that the dark woods keep.
Silent night, with stars above,
Whispers of the world we love.

With each step, the stillness grows,
In nature's arms, the heart bestows.
A moment paused, a fleeting chance,
In winter's breath, we find our dance.

Tranquil Flurries Dance

Snowflakes twirl in gentle grace,
Dancing softly, interlace.
A symphony of white confetti,
Cascading, light and ready.

Breath of wind, a subtle sigh,
Touching cheeks as cold winds fly.
Each flurry sings a soft refrain,
In winter's heart, no room for pain.

Children laugh and spin about,
Joyful echoes, winter's shout.
Sleds and laughter fill the air,
A rapture found, beyond compare.

In stillness, snowflakes kiss the earth,
A moment's pause, reflective worth.
As twilight settles, colors blend,
In tranquil flurries, time will bend.

With every flake that meets the ground,
A new beginning, life unbound.
Winter's art, a fleeting chance,
In peaceful moments, hearts can dance.

A Quiet Embrace of Frost

Morning glimmers, frost adorns,
Nature wakes in silent yawns.
Every blade, a crystal crown,
Winter's breath, its soft renown.

Whispers drift in muted glow,
A tranquil hush, the world moves slow.
Crisp and clear, the air does sing,
In quietude, new life springs.

Gentle hands of frost embrace,
Each corner holds a tender trace.
Beneath the icy, silver lace,
A world transformed, a sacred space.

Time stands still; the moment's near,
To savor all that winter clears.
Embracing warmth, a soft ignite,
In quiet nights, the stars burn bright.

Breathless whispers, nature's art,
A frozen moment, close to heart.
In winter's chill, we pause and breathe,
A quiet grace, our hearts believe.

The Gentle Hand of Winter

Winter's touch, a soft caress,
Blankets wrap in white excess.
The world adorned, a silent glow,
Beneath a veil of purest snow.

Fingers trace the icy seams,
A hush that cradles all our dreams.
Footprints marked on frozen paths,
Chasing echoes of our laughs.

The air so crisp, it sparkles bright,
Stars peek down, in the soft night.
Each breath released, a steamy plume,
In winter's breath, we find our room.

Nature sleeps, yet hearts awake,
In silence deep, we find what's at stake.
Frosted windows, stories told,
In winter's grip, we turn to gold.

With every gust, a ghostly sweep,
The gentle hand of winter keeps.
Holding dreams in frosty hands,
While time whispers through the lands.

The Silent Language of Winter

The trees stand bare and still,
Whispers of frost in the air.
A blanket of snow covers all,
Nature speaks without a care.

Footsteps muffled beneath the quilt,
Echoes of silence softly play.
The world is hushed, calm, serene,
As winter claims the day.

The sky drapes low, a muted gray,
Horizon blends with the cold ground.
In stillness, life takes a pause,
The quiet of peace profound.

With every flake, a story falls,
Memories held in frozen grace.
The world turns white, pure and bright,
In winter's calm embrace.

Under the moon's soft glow,
Shadows dance on frosted skin.
The night sky holds a sacred hush,
While dreams in silence spin.

Hushed Reflections on the White

A world transformed by gentle snow,
Mirrored in shades of soft light.
Each breath hangs in the chilly air,
As day yields to tranquil night.

Footprints mark the untouched field,
Stories untold, waiting to share.
In the stillness, time stands still,
Embrace the beauty, stop and stare.

Silent reflections upon the ground,
Nature's artistry on display.
Each flake a treasure, a fleeting gem,
A reminder of nature's way.

Crisp whispers in the twilight glow,
Soft sighs of the gently falling.
Every breath feels like a prayer,
In winter's beauty, we find enthralling.

Feathers Falling from the Sky

As snowflakes drift from clouds above,
Like feathers falling from the sky.
Each flake unique, a silent gift,
Whirling down without a sigh.

The earth adorned in white soft lace,
Nature's blanket, pure and wide.
Each moment sparkles with delight,
In winter's arms, we must abide.

A canvas of dreams awaits us here,
Each flake a whisper, soft and clear.
They twirl and dance on winter's breath,
A ballet of silence, drawing near.

In wonder, we watch as the world transforms,
Under the spell of the chilly night.
These gentle gifts from above descend,
In beauty, we find our light.

Secrets in the Powdered Blanket

The earth lies soft, a powdered sheet,
Hidden stories lie beneath.
With each snowfall, whispers blend,
In silence thick, we find our breath.

Footsteps pause on the winter's stage,
Secrets buried, waiting to unfold.
In the blanket's hush, we listen close,
To tales of warmth in the cold.

The air is crisp, alive with dreams,
With muffled laughter, secrets shared.
As night descends, shadows gather,
In winter's hush, we are ensnared.

Frosted patterns trace the ground,
Every flake a note in time.
In the quiet, mysteries linger,
In the heart, a gentle rhyme.

Through the night, whispers echo low,
In the snow, we find our way.
The world transformed beneath our feet,
In winter's embrace, we choose to stay.

Beneath a Blanket of Frost

The morning light creeps slow,
While the world is wrapped in white,
Each blade of grass aglow,
A sparkling, frosty sight.

Whispers of winter's chill,
Rest upon the silent ground,
Nature's breath, so still,
Echoes in a shimmering sound.

Glistening trees stand tall,
Crystals hanging from each branch,
Soft as a snowflake's fall,
In this frozen, quiet dance.

Footsteps on the icy trail,
Crunching softly, one by one,
In this peaceful fairy tale,
The day has just begun.

As the sun begins to rise,
Painting gold upon the white,
Nature opens its wise eyes,
Greeting us with pure delight.

Whispers Carried by the Wind

Through the trees a secret flies,
Dancing softly, free and light,
In the evening's gentle sighs,
Whispers fade into the night.

The moonbeams catch the breeze,
Underneath the starry skies,
Carrying tales of the seas,
Where the waves tell lullabies.

Each rustle speaks a truth,
From the forest to the glade,
In the stillness, there's youth,
Hidden in the paths we made.

Words unspoken fill the air,
Wrapped in shadows, dreams alive,
Every breath, a heart laid bare,
In this moment, we can thrive.

As the dawn begins to break,
Hope emerges, fresh and bright,
In each whisper, choices wake,
Guiding us toward the light.

The Breezy Breath of Serenity

A gentle touch upon the skin,
Breath of nature, sweet and pure,
In the silence, peace begins,
Calming hearts with soothing cure.

Leaves are swaying, soft and slow,
Dancing lightly with the air,
In this moment, time unfolds,
And worries vanish into rare.

Ripples on the tranquil lake,
Reflecting whispers of the sky,
Every wave a soft embrace,
As the moments slip on by.

In the garden, colors bloom,
Fragrance mingles with the breeze,
Wrapped in nature's sweet perfume,
Finding calm among the trees.

As twilight paints the world anew,
A canvas filled with shades of peace,
In this breath, our spirits grew,
In serene beauty, we find release.

A Symphony in Pale

The world is cloaked in shades of gray,
Muted tones of soft embrace,
A subtle tune begins to play,
In each quiet, tranquil space.

Snowflakes dance, a gentle waltz,
Falling down like whispered dreams,
Natures canvas, pure results,
Flowing softly in bright streams.

Chimes of icicles ring clear,
Harmonies of winter's song,
In the silence, we can hear,
Where we truly all belong.

As the twilight draws us near,
Light and shadow intertwine,
Every moment crystal clear,
In this symphony divine.

So let us linger in the grace,
Of winter's magic, soft and pale,
In this peaceful, cherished place,
We find harmony in detail.

Whispers of Winter's Veil

Silent snowflakes gently dance,
Beneath the pale moon's glance.
Trees wear coats of gleaming white,
As shadows fade into the night.

Hushed tones of the swirling breeze,
Cradle dreams among the trees.
Footsteps muffled, lost in time,
Rhythms of a winter rhyme.

Frosted whispers, secrets shared,
In the stillness, souls are bared.
Candles flicker, warm and bright,
Guiding hearts through the cold night.

Stars like diamonds, twinkling high,
Underneath the velvet sky.
Each breath visible in the air,
A testament to hope and care.

Embers glow, a fire near,
As laughter echoes, sweet and clear.
In winter's arms, we find our peace,
In whispered dreams, all worries cease.

Frosted Dreams Float Down

Glistening whispers on the ground,
Frosted dreams begin to surround.
Each flake tells a tale of old,
In shimmering blankets, stories unfold.

Gentle breezes bring a chill,
Filling night with a tranquil thrill.
Eager hearts crave the serene,
In the silence, magic seen.

Pine trees sway with sleepy grace,
Nature dons a crystal lace.
Moonlit paths weave through the night,
Guiding souls with tender light.

Crisp air dances on skin,
Winter's song invites us in.
In the hush, we close our eyes,
Listening to the starlit sighs.

As dawn breaks with a blush of gold,
New day whispers stories untold.
In frosted dreams, we find our way,
Embracing the magic of each day.

Crystal Shrouds in Stillness

A crystal shroud envelops the land,
In frozen beauty, nature planned.
Each branch decorated, pure and bright,
Cradles the quiet of the night.

Rustling leaves in a gentle sigh,
Echo whispers of days gone by.
Underneath the silver glow,
Memories linger, soft and slow.

Frosty patterns paint the glass,
Eager moments as they pass.
Sunrise breaks with pastel hues,
Wrapping the earth in tender cues.

With each breath, the world stands still,
Heartbeats blend with winter's chill.
In the stillness, we reflect,
In crystal dreams, we connect.

Together, we hold this fleeting time,
In silence, our spirits climb.
For in winter's embrace, we find
The gentle warmth of heart and mind.

A Still Canvas of Nature

In the forest deep and wide,
Colors blend, where dreams abide.
Leaves whisper stories, soft and low,
As the gentle rivers flow.

Mountains rise, a mighty wall,
Guarding secrets, standing tall.
Sunlight dances on the streams,
Painting light within our dreams.

Flowers bloom in vibrant grace,
Nature's art, a warm embrace.
Each petal holds a tale to share,
Of the beauty held with care.

Silent winds through branches sway,
Guiding thoughts along the way.
Every step, a moment pure,
In this realm, we all endure.

At dusk, the sky ignites with fire,
A canvas born from night's desire.
Stars emerge, the world in sleep,
Nature's promise, calm and deep.

The Subtle Call of Winter's Breath

Crystals glisten on the ground,
Winter's blanket, soft and round.
Breath of cold, a silent sigh,
Whispers secrets as they fly.

Branches bare, in silence stand,
Chasing warmth from distant lands.
Frosted patterns on the glass,
Nature stretches, slow and vast.

Snowflakes dance in gentle grace,
Each a wish from a hidden place.
Lanterns glow with golden light,
Summoning magic through the night.

Footsteps crunch on frozen ground,
Every sound a haunting sound.
In the air, a crisp embrace,
Winter's spirit fills the space.

Nights are long, the world is still,
Time to pause, to dream, to chill.
Nature's heart beats soft and slow,
In the hush, a warmth will grow.

Muted Melodies of the Night

Moonlight drapes the world in silk,
Whispers weave like softest milk.
Stars hold secrets in their gleam,
Crafting stories, bright with dream.

Crickets sing their twilight song,
In the dark, where shadows throng.
A gentle breeze, a lover's sigh,
Humming tunes that drift and fly.

Night unfolds with veiled embrace,
A quiet calm, a sacred space.
Every moment, thick with grace,
Magic swirls in hidden place.

Dreamers roam through starlit skies,
Chasing traces of their highs.
In the dark, the heart takes flight,
To dance along the edge of night.

Moonbeams flicker, softly cast,
Painting shadows that will last.
In this world, where echoes blend,
Muted melodies transcend.

Cacophony in Hush

In the quiet, chaos reigns,
Silent thunder, soft refrains.
Colors clash beneath the dome,
A symphony of roots and loam.

Whispers clash like waves on shore,
Every hush, a vital score.
Heartbeat drumming through the night,
Anguish mixed with pure delight.

Tension builds in silent room,
A restless dream, a growing bloom.
Echoes clash, create a space,
Harmonies of time and place.

Voices rise, then fade away,
Painting sound in shades of gray.
In this cacophony we find,
The beauty held in every mind.

Moments dance in vibrant strife,
Layered sounds of primal life.
In the hush, we learn to hear,
The chaotic truth that draws us near.

Soft Secrets in the Chill

Whispers weave through frosty air,
Dance of shadows, soft and rare.
Underneath the pale moon's glow,
Heartbeats echo, soft and slow.

Silent wishes drift and sway,
Hidden dreams in cold's ballet.
Each breath lingers, crisp and bright,
Soft secrets held within the night.

Gentle snowflakes kiss the ground,
Nature's hush, a calming sound.
Frosted whispers, tender grace,
Where time pauses in its pace.

Stars emerge in velvet skies,
Shimmering truths through frosted sighs.
In this realm of dreams anew,
The heart finds peace, calm and true.

Amidst the chill, we find our way,
In soft secrets that softly play.
Wrapped in stillness, we belong,
In the night's sweet, silent song.

Dreamscapes Wrapped in White

Fields of snow, a soft embrace,
Nature dons a wintry lace.
Hushed horizons blend and glide,
In dreamscapes where we softly bide.

Peaceful whispers in the snow,
Guiding hearts like rivers flow.
Every flake, a story spun,
A tapestry of all we've won.

Moonlit paths that gently shine,
Tracing steps through realms divine.
Footprints fade in silver light,
In this world, our spirits light.

Clouds drift low, a curtain fine,
Dreams unfold, a secret sign.
Wrapped in white, we find our grace,
In winter's arms, a warm embrace.

As dawn breaks through, the colors bloom,
Awakening life from winter's gloom.
In this dreamscape, hearts take flight,
Two souls dance till morning light.

An Echo of Echoes

In the forest, whispers play,
Echoes linger, fade away.
Voices of the past resound,
In this space, we're tightly bound.

A melody from ages old,
Stories vibrant, truths unfold.
Lost in thoughts of what has been,
In echoes where our dreams begin.

Footsteps trace the paths we share,
Time's reflections fill the air.
Moments captured, softly thrown,
In the woods, we're never alone.

Shadows dance beneath the trees,
Every rustle, gentle breeze.
Nature holds the tales so dear,
An echo of our laughter here.

As dusk unveils the stars up high,
We find solace in the sky.
In echoes of the night, we sing,
The past remains; it's everything.

The Quietude of Crystal Nights

Crystal nights in silver glow,
Whispers drift with softest flow.
In the stillness, dreams take flight,
Cradled close in serene night.

Moonbeams dance on frozen streams,
Weaving softly through our dreams.
Wrapped in warmth of night's soft sigh,
Stars like diamonds in the sky.

Shadows stretch under soft light,
Embraced within this tranquil sight.
Every heartbeat, every breath,
In this stillness, we find rest.

Gentle frost, a tender caress,
In the quiet, we are blessed.
Each moment lingers, pure and bright,
A reflection of the night.

Time stands still in crystal air,
In the magic, we both dare.
To lose ourselves, to seek anew,
In the quiet, I find you.

Hushed Echoes of Frost

Whispers of chill in the morn,
Nature adorns with frost's crown.
Each blade of grass, gently worn,
Glistens like jewels in the town.

Silent shadows stretch and creep,
Under the gaze of the pale sun.
Winter's embrace, a secret to keep,
Wrapped in stillness, all is one.

Birds concealed in their nest,
Await the warmth of spring's call.
In icy silence, they rest,
While the soft snowflakes gently fall.

Footsteps muffled, the world slows,
As nature holds her breath tight.
In this hushed white, beauty glows,
Under the watch of the starry night.

Each heartbeat echoes the frost,
In this canvas, crisp and clear.
Moments cherished, never lost,
As winter whispers in our ear.

The Soft Blanket Descends

Clouds gather, a soft whisper,
As twilight bends to embrace night.
Gentle flakes begin to stir,
Falling around, a shimmering sight.

A soft blanket, warm and white,
Hides the earth beneath its fold.
Snowflakes dance in soft twilight,
Stories of winter, timeless and bold.

Crystalline dreams in the air,
Covering streets like a song.
Each flake unique, beyond compare,
In this peace, we all belong.

The world slows down, hushed and still,
Soft laughter echoes from nearby.
Snowman forming on the hill,
Under the soft blanket, shy.

Cocoas warmed by the flame,
Gathering friends, tales to weave.
In soft embrace, we find our aim,
In winter's magic, we believe.

When the World Holds Its Breath

In the depth of winter's grasp,
Time stands still, a silent cheer.
The world awaits, a quiet gasp,
As nature whispers, crystal clear.

Branches weigh down with snow's kiss,
Frosty breath paints the air cold.
In this wonder, there's pure bliss,
A story in silence unfolds.

Footprints lead through a white maze,
Each step echoes like a prayer.
Underneath the frosty glaze,
The earth sleeps gently, unaware.

Stars twinkle in the night sky,
As dreams drift on winter's tide.
Under the moon's watchful eye,
Frozen moments from which we bide.

With every sigh, we draw near,
Wrapped in warmth of love's embrace.
When the world holds its breath, we hear,
The heartbeats of time in this place.

Veils of White Upon the Earth

Veils of white upon the earth,
A canvas stretched, pure and bright.
In the quiet, we find worth,
As snowflakes weave secrets at night.

Each flake falls with graceful ease,
A shimmering touch in the dark.
Nature's cloak, a gentle tease,
Breathes life into each frozen spark.

Trees stand tall, adorned with grace,
As branches bow through winter's charm.
In this snowy, serene space,
The world emerges, calm and warm.

Children laugh with joyful delight,
As they sculpt dreams from white fields.
While time shifts into soft twilight,
In this magic, the heart yields.

Under the veils of winter's breath,
We find hope in each drifting flake.
Through the silence conquering death,
A heart reborn with each dawn's wake.

Winter's Gentle Palette

Softly falls the purest snow,
Blanketing the world below.
Branches draped in white delight,
Nature whispers, calm and bright.

Frozen streams that quietly flow,
Beneath the frost, a gentle glow.
Silent nights with skies so clear,
Winter's charm is always near.

Footprints mark the untouched ground,
Echoes of a world profound.
Every flake a work of art,
Nature's canvas, pure and smart.

Winter winds that softly sigh,
A lullaby beneath the sky.
Colors fade in muted light,
Yet in stillness, hearts take flight.

Traces of Slumbering Life

Beneath the snow, a heartbeat lies,
Dreaming softly, where silence sighs.
Roots that twine in Earth's embrace,
Waiting for the sun's warm grace.

Each tiny seed, a secret held,
In the cold, their dreams repelled.
Life's pulse beats, though still and shy,
Quiet realms where whispers fly.

Crystals gleam like frozen tears,
Holding close the dormant years.
Nature rests in peaceful schemes,
Cradled softly in her dreams.

When spring calls, the thaw will sing,
Reviving every living thing.
Yet for now, in hushed repose,
Traces of life gently doze.

Hidden Stories Beneath the Ice

Underneath the icy sheets,
Ancient tales where time retreats.
Fossils trapped in winter's grip,
Memories in silence sip.

Cracks and crevices reveal,
Fragments of a history real.
Each layer tells of life that thrived,
In winter's hold, stillness derived.

Cold reflections, shadows cast,
Echoes from a distant past.
Whispers of the softest breeze,
Carried on with perfect ease.

Mysterious depths unseen,
Guarding secrets, pure and keen.
In icy prisons, stories lie,
Waiting for the thaw to try.

Shadows Cast by the Moonlight Glow

In the night, a silver sheen,
Bathe the world in midnight dream.
Moonbeams dance through every tree,
Whispers float on calm, dark sea.

Shadows stretch across the land,
Mysterious and softly planned.
Harboring the night's soft grace,
In the stillness, secrets trace.

Gentle breezes sigh and stir,
Telling tales of what occurred.
A quiet peace enfolds the earth,
In moonlight's glow, rebirth and mirth.

Stars align in perfect view,
Stitching dreams in shades of blue.
As night unfolds, let spirits fly,
In shadows cast, the heart will lie.

Clarity in a World Wrapped in White

In a sea of white, I stand still,
Each snowflake whispers, a soft thrill.
The air holds secrets, crisp and clear,
With every breath, winter draws near.

Branches hold treasures, pure and bright,
Glistening softly in the pale light.
A moment suspended, time feels slow,
In this tranquil realm, the soul can grow.

Footsteps echo on the blanket deep,
In silence, the world seems to sleep.
The sun peeks shyly, a golden kiss,
In the white expanse, I find my bliss.

Each gust of wind sings a soft tune,
Under the watchful eye of the moon.
In clarity found, I roam and wander,
In this world wrapped in white, I ponder.

A canvas untouched, pure and wide,
In the stillness, I take my stride.
Frozen in time, yet feelings bloom,
In this winter wonder, I find my room.

A Breath Between the Flurries

The sky dances down with flakes of lace,
In this moment, I find my place.
A stillness falls, the chaos retreats,
Between the flurries, my heart beats.

Glistening whispers, secrets shared,
In this winter's grasp, I am bared.
The world slows down, a gentle sigh,
As I watch the snowflakes tumble and fly.

Crisp air tinged with winter's chill,
Each breath I take, a quiet thrill.
In the pause of storms, I feel alive,
In the waltz of the snow, I thrive.

With every flurry, dreams take flight,
A breath, a pause, in the fading light.
In this fleeting moment, I find grace,
Between the flurries, a sacred space.

Lingering soft, the winter night,
In the hush of snow, all is right.
A breath of peace, a gentle sigh,
A balm for the soul, as dreams drift by.

Frozen Dances of the Night

The stars shimmer bright in the velvet sky,
As the moon whispers secrets, low and sly.
Snowflakes twirl in an elegant dance,
In the frozen night, I take a chance.

The world transforms under the silver glow,
In the quiet of night, emotions flow.
Each step I take, the earth creaks slow,
As I join in the dance, feeling the glow.

Shadowed whispers in the swirling air,
A melody lingers, sweet and rare.
In the cold embrace, warmth takes flight,
Lost in the moment, the frozen night.

With each twirl, the silence breaks,
In the leaps and bounds, my spirit wakes.
The chill wraps around like a lover's sigh,
Dancing with dreams as the hours fly.

Under the starlit, shimmering sea,
I find my heart, wild and free.
In the frozen dances, I lose all fright,
And become one with the magical night.

The Quiet Blanket's Shimmer

Softly laid, a blanket bright,
Covering the earth in purest white.
A quilt of silence, vast and wide,
Where dreams and peace effortlessly hide.

The gentle shimmer, a soft glow,
In this stillness, time is slow.
Each flake a story, unique and bold,
In this quiet world, warmth unfolds.

Footprints mark paths in the glistening sea,
As I wander through this reverie.
Underneath the frosty dome,
In this tranquil realm, I find my home.

A crisp embrace in the twilight hush,
In nature's arms, there's no rush.
The quiet blanket holds me tight,
A shelter of calm in the lengthy night.

With every sigh, the world feels small,
In this shimmering peace, I stand tall.
Wrapped in the magic, I inhale deep,
The quiet blanket, my heart to keep.

Ecstasy in a White Abyss

In silence deep, the world transforms,
As snowflakes dance, in crisp, cold forms.
A canvas white, so pure, so vast,
Each flake a whisper, a spell that's cast.

With every breath, the chill ignites,
A thrill that swells in winter nights.
In nature's grip, joy feels so near,
An ecstasy found, without a fear.

Footprints fade in the snowy embrace,
Time stands still in this tranquil space.
The heart leaps high, unbound, alive,
In every flake, the soul will thrive.

Under the stars, the night unfolds,
Tales of warmth in the bitter cold.
In this abyss, a joy unmasked,
In every flurry, love is tasked.

Awake in dreams, the snowflakes twirl,
A symphony sweet in a frozen whirl.
Ecstasy found in a white expanse,
In this quiet realm, we weave romance.

Ghostly Prints on Familiar Trails

Footsteps linger on paths we know,
Ghostly prints in the soft white glow.
Each mark a story, a memory's trace,
Whispers of laughter in this sacred space.

Through woods enchanted, the shadows weave,
In every turn, a tale to believe.
Familiar trails, yet eerily new,
Where echoes of past begin to accrue.

The winter's breath carries secrets old,
In frosty silence, the heart feels bold.
Every crunch of snow, a haunting call,
A dance with shadows, weaving through all.

Beneath the moon's watchful sheen,
Ghostly prints tell of sights unseen.
In every step, life's tale unfolds,
In these familiar trails, courage molds.

As dawn breaks bright, the prints may fade,
Yet in our hearts, the memories laid.
Faint impressions on the soul remain,
In ghostly whispers, we'll meet again.

The Tenderness of a Snowy Whim

In fleeting moments, snowflakes sigh,
Soft as whispers beneath the sky.
A tender touch on the earth below,
Each flake a secret, a love to bestow.

Gentle cascades from heavens high,
Like loving gestures, they float and fly.
Embracing the ground in a warm embrace,
The snowy whim brings a tranquil grace.

Children's laughter fills the air,
As snowmen rise, free from all care.
In every drift, a dream set free,
A tapestry spun from the heart's decree.

With every flurry, joy intertwines,
In the snowy dance, the spirit shines.
A world transformed in delicate hues,
In tenderness wrapped, our hearts renew.

As twilight falls, the silence deepens,
In snowy whispers, the heart often weeps.
The softest touch of winter's kiss,
A snowy whim, a promise of bliss.

Softly Woven Winter Wonders

In faded light, the world aglow,
Winter wonders begin to show.
Glistening blankets of purest white,
Softly woven through the night.

Trees stand tall, adorned so bright,
Each branch a gem in the soft moonlight.
Nature's quilt, so warm, divine,
In the stillness, our dreams align.

Whispers of winds through frosty lanes,
Each breath a story, a dance remains.
Magic thrives where the cold winds play,
In woven wonders, we lose our way.

As dusk descends, the stars ignite,
A canopy of dreams in the frosty night.
Every twinkle a tale, a gentle spell,
In the tapestry of winter, we dwell.

In this embrace, we find our peace,
Softly woven, our joys increase.
Bundled close, our hearts entwined,
In winter's wonders, love is blind.

Journeys in Frosted Stillness

In silence deep, the stars do gleam,
Through whispered paths, we chase a dream.
The night is wrapped in winter's grace,
Each breath a mist, a fleeting trace.

Amidst the trees, the shadows play,
A fragile light will guide the way.
With every step, the world transforms,
In frosted calm, the heart conforms.

The moon, a guardian in the sky,
Watches as we wander by.
In quietude, the spirit soars,
Through frozen realms and hidden doors.

Soft whispers break the chilling air,
Stories linger everywhere.
With every footfall, memories bloom,
In nature's clasp, dispelling gloom.

Journeys taken, paths anew,
In frosted stillness, hearts are true.
Embrace the night, the chill, the glow,
For in this peace, true wonders flow.

Echoes of a Crystal Night

Beneath the sky with twinkling lights,
We roam through echoes of the night.
Each step a crunch, a soft refrain,
In moonlit dreams, we break the chain.

The air is crisp, alive with sound,
Each whisper of the wind profound.
In crystal shards, the world is cast,
Moments shimmer, shadows past.

Frosted branches, diamonds reside,
A tapestry where secrets hide.
We dance in snow, a fleeting fate,
Embracing the chill, we hesitate.

Stars are scattered, timeless and bright,
Guiding dreams through the endless night.
In every breath, the past Ignites,
We find ourselves in crystal nights.

As dawn approaches, colors blend,
The echoes fade, yet they transcend.
In memories, the magic stays,
Through winter's heart, our spirits blaze.

The Serene Caress of Winter

Softly falls the snow at dusk,
In white embrace, the world feels husk.
With every flake, a tale untold,
In winter's arms, we find the bold.

Nature whispers, calm and low,
In tranquil hush, the soft winds flow.
A gentle touch, a frosty breath,
In serene caress, we flirt with death.

The pines adorned in silver lace,
Stand sentinel in time and space.
In quietude, our thoughts align,
With every sigh, the stars entwine.

Moments linger, suspended grace,
In winter's hold, we find our place.
We lean into the winter chill,
And in that peace, our hearts are still.

The world reclaims its tranquil song,
In winter's embrace, we belong.
Through icy nights and frosted beams,
We find our solace in snowbound dreams.

Frozen Reveries Undisturbed

In stillness deep, the world takes pause,
A frozen realm with quiet laws.
Each flake that falls a memory made,
In silent whispers, dreams won't fade.

The lakes are mirrors of the moon,
Reflecting hope with every tune.
As shadows dance in crystal light,
We find our place in the heart of night.

Frosted meadows, whispers recall,
Echoes of laughter, a cherished call.
With every breath, a moment caught,
In reveries where warmth is sought.

The branches bow with weighty grace,
Nature's canvas, a serene space.
Through frozen paths, our spirits roam,
In undisturbed, we feel at home.

The world may sleep, but in the dream,
We wander forth, a soft, bright beam.
Amidst the frost, our hearts will bind,
In frozen reveries, love you'll find.

The Tranquil Touch of Twilight

As daylight fades to quiet hues,
The stars begin their soft debut.
A gentle breeze in whispers spoke,
Embracing night with calm, bespoke.

The sky adorned with shades of blue,
Awakens dreams in every view.
In twilight's grace, the world stands still,
A tranquil touch that time will fill.

The moon arises, silver bright,
Casting shadows, soft as light.
The peace of dusk, a warm embrace,
In every heart, finds its place.

A hush descends on earth so wide,
While nature breathes with gentle pride.
In twilight's arms, we softly sway,
Awaiting dreams to light the way.

The stars will guide our distant thoughts,
In tranquil moments, time is sought.
With every breath, the world will pause,
In the twilight's gentle cause.

The Whispering Woods Under Rest

Beneath the boughs where shadows play,
The whispering woods in soft decay.
Leaves murmur secrets, old and wise,
In every rustle, nature sighs.

A carpet laid of moss and green,
The forest floor, a tranquil scene.
Each step unfolds a story told,
In whispers of the brave and bold.

The ancient trees, guardians still,
In quietude, they share their will.
Among the roots, a world unseen,
Where dreams entwine in emerald sheen.

The twilight glow begins to creep,
As lovers of the night awake.
In every nook, the shadows blend,
A whispered promise, hearts ascend.

The peace of night envelops deep,
In quiet woods, our thoughts to keep.
With every breath of fragrant air,
The whispering woods show us care.

Echoes of Softness in the Dark

In silence deep, the night unfolds,
With echoes soft, as the dark enfolds.
A lullaby of shadows plays,
In tender whispers, softly sways.

The moonlight spills on gentle ground,
With every breath, a peace profound.
Night creatures stir, in shadows cast,
In echoes of the day gone past.

The stars above, they twinkle bright,
While dreams take flight in the gentle night.
With each soft sound, a heart takes pause,
In echoes' depth, we find our cause.

The world retreats, a quiet state,
In darkness wrapped, we meditate.
The softness calls, a sweet embrace,
In echoing night, we find our place.

As time drifts on, we learn to listen,
To whispers soft, and dreams that glisten.
In shadows deep, we find our spark,
With echoes of softness in the dark.

The Gentle Kiss of Ice

In winters grasp, a blanket white,
The gentle kiss of ice, a sight.
With frosty breath upon the trees,
The world is hushed in tranquil freeze.

Each crystal glimmers in the glow,
Of morning light, a radiant show.
Footsteps crunch on frozen ground,
In winter's hold, a peace profound.

The air is crisp, the silence near,
As whispers of the cold appear.
In nature's charm, we find our bliss,
In every flake, a fleeting kiss.

The world now wrapped in chilly lace,
Each breath we take, a fleeting race.
The gentle touch of winter's night,
In dreams, we dance 'neath silver light.

As twilight fades, the day will cease,
In snowy realms, we find our peace.
The gentle kiss of ice will stay,
In memories warm, come what may.

Poetry Adrift on Winter's Breath

Whispers glide on frosty winds,
Softly carrying tales untold.
Each breath a moment lingers,
In frozen hues, memories unfold.

Branches draped in silvery light,
Crystals dance in moonlit grace.
A canvas bright, cloaked in night,
As silence wraps the world's embrace.

Footsteps muffled on the ground,
Echoes fade into the white.
A heartbeat's pulse, barely found,
Wrapped in the warmth of winter's might.

The sky drips soft, a tender sigh,
With every flake, a story spun.
Moments fall, they do not die,
Yet linger long after they're done.

In this hush, dreams gently weave,
A tapestry of hope and glow.
Winter's breath, we dare believe,
In poetry's embrace, we grow.

Fragments of Frost in Still Air

Brittle shards in morning light,
Each one a glimpse of fleeting time.
Nature's art, a pure delight,
Captured in winter's quiet rhyme.

Glistening fields, a soft expanse,
Beneath the shadowed, looming trees.
Every crystal holds a chance,
A world transformed by winter's freeze.

Voices lost in shimmers bright,
Echoes dance on winds that flow.
In the stillness, hearts take flight,
As stories in the frost bestow.

Threads of silver weave the air,
Ember eyes find warmth in cold.
In each breath, a poet's prayer,
Woven with dreams and tales retold.

A single flake, rare and pure,
Carried on a sighing breeze.
In this moment, hearts are sure,
Finding solace in winter's tease.

A Blanket for the Quiet Land

Softly falls the snow at dawn,
A blanket white for earth to lace.
Each flake a whisper, crisp and drawn,
   Embracing stillness in its grace.

Fields of white, a hush profound,
   Footprints trace a hidden tale.
Every corner, every mound,
Wrapped in peace, where dreams prevail.

Rustling leaves now silent stand,
As nature holds its breath in awe.
Winter drapes its gentle hand,
Over the world, a calming law.

Time seems to pause in soft repose,
Moments linger, stretched and wide.
In this scene, the heart bestows,
Tender warmth, where hopes abide.

Textures new beneath the frost,
A canvas pure, untouched by strife.
In winter's realm, never lost,
We find the essence of true life.

Layers of Quietude in White

Veils of snow, a silent shroud,
Cloaking whispers, soft and deep.
In winter's arms, we are bowled,
To find the stillness that we seek.

Each breath taken, crisp and clear,
Moments drift like clouds above.
Wrapped in layers, love draws near,
In soft embraces, warmth and love.

Skies adorned with ashen light,
Glimmers hint at day's gentle birth.
Through this realm, we take our flight,
Finding solace in winter's mirth.

The world enwrapped in purest white,
Shields our hearts from every care.
In quietude, wrongs set right,
As peace and beauty fill the air.

Here we stroll through realms so calm,
Wrapped in dreams, beneath the sky.
Winter soothes with its sweet psalm,
In silent layers, we comply.

Hallowed Grounds of Frost

In hallowed grounds where frost does lay,
The whispering winds softly play,
Each crystal shard, a story told,
Nature's beauty, pure and bold.

Beneath the trees, a silence dwells,
Where winter's magic gently swells,
The light of dawn, a golden hue,
Envelops all in frosty blue.

The ground is still, a frozen bed,
Where dreams of spring have gently fled,
A moment caught in time's embrace,
A serene and sacred space.

As shadows dance on icy streams,
Awake beneath the sun's soft beams,
With every breath, the cold ignites,
A symphony of winter's rites.

The world transformed, a glistening sight,
In hallowed grounds of pure delight,
With every flake, a gentle sound,
A tale of peace in frost is found.

Mysteries Beneath the Snow Cover

Beneath the snow, the secrets lie,
Whispers carried on the sigh,
A world concealed, yet full of grace,
In icy realms, we softly trace.

The branches bow with heavy loads,
While hidden paths weave winter's roads,
Each step a quest, each drift a clue,
To mysteries that still feel new.

Frozen streams and silent glades,
Where every shape the snow cascades,
In quiet dreams, the stories flow,
Of life beneath the frosty glow.

The stillness holds a magic rare,
With every breath, an icy air,
The world awaits a thawing sun,
To stir the life that's just begun.

In winter's grasp, the hints reside,
Of nature's dance with time as guide,
Each flake a part of mysteries spun,
Beneath the snow, the tales are won.

Frosty Grace Enjoys the Quiet

In frosty grace, the world lies still,
A blanket soft on vale and hill,
The quiet whispers, nature's song,
In winter's heart, we all belong.

The trees stand tall, like sentinels,
In crystal coats, their presence swells,
While silvered branches catch the light,
In frosty grace, the day turns bright.

Each breath of air, a chilling kiss,
A moment caught, a fleeting bliss,
With every glance, the beauty grows,
In tranquil scenes where silence flows.

The world transforms, a wondrous art,
With frosty grace, it warms the heart,
In nature's arms, we find our peace,
A quiet joy that will not cease.

As dusk descends, the stars arise,
In frosty grace, the night complies,
With silvered dreams, we drift away,
In winter's hush, we long to stay.

Celestial White Adornments

The celestial white adorns the night,
With stars that twinkle, pure and bright,
A canvas vast, where dreams take flight,
In winter's grasp, we feel the light.

Each flake a spark, a world to cherish,
In twilight's glow, the shadows perish,
A wondrous scene of beauty spun,
Where silent wishes become one.

The moonlight dances on the snow,
A silken path where soft winds blow,
Each glimmer speaks of tales untold,
In celestial white, the night unfolds.

With twilight's breath, the moment sings,
Of frosty grace and edging wings,
In wonderland, the heart will find,
The beauty held within the mind.

To linger here, in peace we stand,
In celestial white, hand in hand,
The night is wrapped in soft embrace,
A heavenly touch, a sacred space.

Ghosts of Winter's Chill

Whispers roam through barren trees,
Leaves lie curled, with gentle ease.
Footsteps muffled, snowflakes fall,
Nature holds its breath, enthralled.

Silhouettes in twilight's grasp,
Frosty fingers softly clasp.
Echoes of a world once bright,
Fade into the quiet night.

In the shadows, phantoms tread,
On the paths that spirits led.
Every gust, a tale retold,
In the frost, their stories hold.

Frozen streams in silence flow,
Time stands still where cold winds blow.
Moonlight dances on the drift,
Winter's grace, a haunting gift.

Yet hope glimmers in the dark,
Beneath the chill, there's a spark.
From the frost, new life will spring,
Ghosts of winter's chill take wing.

The Calm Before the Storm

Stillness hangs in heavy air,
Birds retreat, the world lays bare.
Clouds thicken, shadows grow,
Nature's heart beats soft and low.

Whispers of the wind take flight,
Faintest hints of coming night.
Leaves rustle in anxious dance,
Waiting for the storm's advance.

A silence wraps the weary ground,
Every heartbeat echoes sound.
Tension builds, a promise near,
As the skies draw ever sheer.

Branches sway, a warning sign,
Nature's pulse, a steady line.
Breath held tight, a world in pause,
Ready for the storm's applause.

Hopeful hearts and heavy sighs,
Beneath the calm, the future lies.
Before the chaos breaks the norm,
We find peace in the coming storm.

Tranquil Tapestry of Ice

Glistening like a silver lace,
Nature's canvas, a frozen space.
Sparkling gems on branches cling,
Winter weaves its quiet spring.

Crystals form on a windowpane,
Frigid art that holds no pain.
Each shard tells a tale of frost,
Of beauty found, but never lost.

Underneath this tranquil guise,
Life still pulses, even lies.
Roots entwined in chilling ground,
Silent strength where hope is found.

Every drip of melting snow,
Signals life will surely grow.
From this tapestry will spring,
Splendor born from winter's sting.

In the hush, a promise waits,
Spring returns as frost abates.
Tranquil moments invite we see,
The peace of winter's symphony.

The Quiet Dance of Light

Sunrise spills its golden hue,
Softly waking worlds anew.
Shadows stretch and slowly sway,
Dancing through the quiet day.

In the hush of dawn's embrace,
Light caresses nature's face.
Whispers of a gentle breeze,
Carry laughter through the trees.

Every ray a fleeting glance,
Painting life in a soft dance.
Moments shimmer, then they fade,
In the light, our dreams are laid.

As twilight waltzes into view,
Stars alight in the sky so blue.
In the calm, we find our peace,
In the night, our worries cease.

For in every flicker bright,
Lives the magic of the night.
In the quiet, we take flight,
As we dance with the fading light.

Murmurs of a Snowy Solstice

Whispers wrap the frozen air,
As silver flakes descend with care.
Each flake a wish, softly spun,
In quiet night, a world begun.

Trees adorned in crystal lace,
Reflecting winter's calm embrace.
Stars above in deep stillness gleam,
While shadows dance in silent dream.

Footsteps hushed on virgin ground,
In this peace, a beauty found.
Nature holds her breath so still,
Time suspended by winter's will.

Glistening paths where moonlight flows,
Through the night, a gentle prose.
Murmurs of stories yet untold,
In frosty breath, the night's unfold.

In the hush, hearts beat as one,
Underneath the watchful sun.
Snowflakes swirl in a waltz so sweet,
A snowy solstice, pure and neat.

Stars Draped in Winter's Calm

In the stillness of the night,
Stars emerge, a wondrous sight.
Draped in velvet, cold and bright,
Whispers echo, pure delight.

Frosty air, a gentle breath,
Hints of magic dance with death.
Each twinkle tells a tale anew,
Of winter's charm and skies so blue.

Pines stand tall in snow's embrace,
Nature's stillness, serene grace.
Underneath the soft moon's light,
Dreams awaken in the night.

Crisp and clear, the world asleep,
In this peace, the heart will keep.
Stars aligned, a guiding voice,
In winter's calm, the soul rejoice.

Echoes of a night divine,
Glistening like the finest wine.
Stars above, like diamonds fall,
In winter's hush, we hear their call.

Loveliness in the Chill of Night

Loveliness in shadows cast,
Paints the sky, a night so vast.
Whispers linger, soft and low,
In the chill, our spirits glow.

Silent dreams on frost-kissed ground,
In the stillness, peace is found.
Moonlight drapes the world in grace,
Every corner, a hidden place.

Stars like lanterns guide the way,
Through the night, where shadows play.
Gentle winds, a lover's sigh,
Beneath the vast and open sky.

Branches bare, but hearts are warm,
Wrapped in winter's quiet charm.
Crisp the air, yet love prevails,
In the night, where joy unveils.

Magic twirls, an endless dance,
In the night, we take our chance.
Loveliness, a fleeting spark,
In the chill, we leave our mark.

A Canvas of White Dreams

A canvas spread with snowy grace,
They paint the world, a soft embrace.
In gentle blush, the dawn awakes,
As winter's hand the silence takes.

Puffs of clouds like cotton float,
On winter's breeze, dreams gently coat.
Each breath a mist, a soft goodbye,
To moments lost, on silent sigh.

White dreams drape the sleeping ground,
In this peace, our hopes are found.
Footprints mark the journey's path,
Through hushed realms, a heart's sweet laugh.

The world transformed, a fairy tale,
In silver light, our worries pale.
Each flake a story wrought from time,
In snowy folds, a gentle rhyme.

A canvas of dreams that softly gleam,
Crafted by a winter's dream.
In this moment, life stands still,
A whispered hope, a winter's thrill.

Silence Carried on the Wind

Whispers float through the tall pine trees,
Gentle currents dance with ease.
A secret shared beneath the moon,
Soft as the night, heartbeats in tune.

Starlight shimmers on the lake,
Mirroring dreams we dare not shake.
Every breath a quiet song,
In the stillness, we belong.

Leaves tremble without a sound,
Echoes of peace all around.
Nature's hush wraps like a shawl,
In this silence, we feel it all.

The world pauses to listen near,
In moments where the heart draws near.
A timeless dance of twilight's grace,
Carried softly through this place.

With every sigh the night unfolds,
Stories shared but never told.
In the silence, we find our way,
Carried forth by winds of sway.

Timeless Beauty in a Frigid Tale

Snowflakes twirling in the air,
Whispers of winter everywhere.
Each flake a story, unique, untold,
Cloaked in silver, a wonder to behold.

Frosty branches, delicate lace,
Nature revels in this icy space.
The world transformed, a glistening sheet,
Every path, a shimmering beat.

In the silence, beauty thrives,
Life concealed in the coldest dives.
A canvas pure, untouched by time,
Each moment crafted, a tender rhyme.

Embers of sunlight pierce the chill,
Painting shadows on the hill.
Glowing warmth in a frosty huddle,
A quiet grace in the winter's cuddle.

Frozen breath in the morning light,
Glimmers of hope in the heart of night.
A timeless dance of ice and flame,
In this stillness, beauty reigns the same.

Nature's Secret Lullaby

Beneath the trees where shadows play,
A whispering breeze leads the way.
Soft like a dream, it drifts and glides,
Cradled softly where peace abides.

The river hums its gentle tune,
In harmony with the silver moon.
Nature's voice, a calming sigh,
Holding secrets as time slips by.

Petals flutter, a tender grace,
In the quiet, they find their place.
A lullaby of earth and sky,
In every leaf, a soft goodbye.

Stars awaken as daylight fades,
Twinkling softly in nature's shades.
Each note a promise, sweet and light,
Heralding peace in the deepening night.

As shadows stretch and moments blend,
Nature's lullaby will never end.
A symphony that stirs the soul,
In every heartbeat, we are whole.

The Choreography of Winter's Gaze

A ballet of snowflakes, swirling high,
Twisting gently from the sky.
Each one unique, a fleeting art,
Dancing softly, a winter's heart.

Cold winds twirl with icy grace,
Painting frost on every face.
Nature holds a masterclass,
In branches bowed and skies of glass.

Moonlight paints the world in white,
Cascading dreams in the still of night.
Every shadow, a silent ghost,
In winter's grasp, we find our host.

The stars blink in with shy applause,
Witnessing nature's quiet cause.
In frozen choreography, time stands still,
As snowflakes dance on the softest hill.

With every gust, the story sways,
In winter's grasp, we learn to praise.
A dance of silence, pure and true,
In the chill of evening, I think of you.

Whispers of Winter's Veil

Snowflakes dance down, soft and light,
Blanketing earth in purest white.
Whispers carried on the chilling breeze,
Silent secrets held among the trees.

Footsteps muffled on a frozen ground,
Nature's tapestry without a sound.
Crystals sparkle, catching the eye,
In winter's arms, the world seems shy.

Fires crackle with warmth and cheer,
While outside, frost paints the year.
Veils of mist in the morning glow,
A tranquil scene, serene and slow.

Branches bow, heavy with snow,
Time stands still, as if to show.
Moments linger in the pale light,
A gentle hush cloaks the night.

Softly falling, the hours wane,
Winter whispers a sweet refrain.
In this embrace, the heart finds peace,
Embracing the stillness, fears release.

Traces of Frosted Dreams

In shadows deep, frost paints the air,
Dreams awaken, tender and rare.
Softest glimmers on fields of white,
Whispers of hopes in the quiet night.

Each breath a cloud, dances and sways,
In the stillness, lost in the maze.
Footprints linger, a story told,
Of winter's magic, brave and bold.

Through cracked windows, the chill creeps in,
A world transformed, where dreams begin.
Glancing back, memories glow,
Frosted paths that lead us slow.

Stars twinkle in the velvet sky,
A canvas for dreams that never die.
In the night's embrace, we find our way,
Carried onward through shadows gray.

With every whisper, the frost will fade,
But the dreams we hold are never played.
Traces of warmth in frozen streams,
Life goes on, wrapped in our dreams.

The Hushed Embrace of White

A blanket laid on the slumbering ground,
Soft and quiet, without a sound.
The hush, a lullaby, softly sings,
Of winter's touch and the peace it brings.

Trees adorned with their crystal crowns,
Glistening bright as the sunlight drowns.
Each flake a story, a whisper's grace,
In the arms of white, we find our place.

Icicles dangle, sharp and clear,
Nature's art, drawing us near.
In this stillness, the heart beats slow,
Wrapped in warmth from the falling snow.

Laughter echoes in the frosty air,
As children play without a care.
Golden firelight flickers and glows,
In winter's arms, our love still grows.

The night is deep, yet spirits soar,
In the quiet, we yearn for more.
A tranquil hug, a gentle sway,
The hushed embrace of the soft white day.

Stillness Beneath the Clouds

Above, the clouds drift, heavy and gray,
Beneath them lies a world at play.
Silent whispers beneath the gloom,
Nature waiting for spring to bloom.

Footsteps echo in the quiet land,
Each touch of frost, cool and grand.
Wrapped in silence, the moments freeze,
Finding solace in the winter's ease.

Hills adorned with a silver sheen,
A picture perfect, yet so serene.
Stillness sways with the gentle sigh,
As fallen leaves wave their goodbye.

The sky may frown, yet hope remains,
In every flake, our joy sustains.
With hearts attuned to the soft embrace,
We wander in this sacred space.

Beneath the clouds, the world stands still,
Nature holds a breath, a timeless thrill.
In wintry landscapes, we find our dreams,
Amidst the stillness, life gently gleams.

Milton Keynes UK
Ingram Content Group UK Ltd.
UKHW021402081224
452111UK00007B/124